Your Journey Within

7 Powerful Steps to Create the Life You Deserve

WISHING YOU LOTS OF
SUCCESS IN YOUR LIFE's
JOURNEY

Love,

Swapna Ambegaonkar

Swapna Ambegaonkar

YOUR JOURNEY WITHIN
http://www.yourjourneywithinbook.com

Copyright © 2017 Swapna Ambegaonkar

ISBN-13: 978-1544812267

Publisher
10-10-10 Publishing
Markham, ON   Canada

Printed in Canada and the United States of America

Contents

Dedication

I would like to dedicate this book to my mentors and coaches.

Acknowledgements

First and foremost, I would like to acknowledge my mentor and coach, Mr. Raymond Aaron, for giving me direction in my life and teaching me the right things at the right time. Raymond, you are one of the most influential people in my life.

I would like to thank my parents, Mr. Manohar Raje and Mrs. Shaila Raje, for supporting me and nurturing me in a very special way. Your love and care have made it possible for me to be what I am today.

I want to acknowledge my mother-in-law, Mrs. Vijaya Ambegaonkar, and my father-in-law, Late Mr. Dilip M. Ambegaonkar, for their confidence in me and their continuous encouragement, which is responsible for my success.

I would like to thank my wonderful husband, Amit, for his unconditional love and unwavering support in all my endeavors, and for being my life partner, sharing many precious moments with me. The encouragement that Amit provides me is so powerful that I am able to achieve much more than I ever thought possible for myself.

I want to thank my two amazing children, my daughter Sanjana and my son, Sahil, for being the reason behind all my achievements, and always being supportive and acting responsibly from very tender ages. I am blessed to have children like you. You make me proud.

I would like to acknowledge my brother Nikhil Raje for being supportive and contributing towards the happiness of our family.

Swapna Ambegaonkar

I would like to thank my sister in law Shilpa Dalvi and her husband Hemant Dalvi, as well as my nieces Pranali Dalvi and Prachiti Dalvi for their continued support and encouragement in areas of my life.

I would like to acknowledge my mentor, Jack Canfield, whose program, *Train The Trainer,* has been life-changing for me. His teachings have had a profound impact, by practically enhancing all aspects of my life.

I want to acknowledge my coaches and mentors, Meir Ezra and Bob Proctor, because of whom I developed the mindset and the courage to be a true entrepreneur. Through their powerful teachings and trainings, I am able to keep on achieving and exceeding my goals.

I want to express my gratitude to all my friends and family, who are always there for me and ready to lend a helping hand whenever I need one. Your willingness to contribute to my success and goals is quite commendable.

I want to acknowledge you, the reader of my book, for taking the time out from your schedule to make a difference in your life. I want to assure you that if you apply even some of the principles in this book, you will see a huge difference in your life and business. These are the exact principles that I use myself, and which have enormously helped my clients to achieve success.

About the Author

Swapna is very passionate about helping others and making a difference in the world by inspiring, encouraging and empowering individuals.

Swapna has the natural ability to connect with you and helps you identify your life purpose and goals. Through this book, she guides and inspires you to be at your best and reach new heights, using practical and real world examples and exercises.

Swapna has been involved in self-development for many years, and truly understands the importance of having the right mindset to be successful in life. She truly believes that the power is in you, and that you can achieve all the goals you have ever wanted to achieve.

Swapna believes in the practical application of knowledge, and also emphasizes the importance of taking action to achieve the life that you deserve.

Success is not just a destination, it is a journey, and Swapna empowers you with powerful and simple steps that you need to take in order to be successful.

Foreword

Swapna Ambegaonkar has put forth very powerful steps that you can take to make a huge difference in your life. *Your Journey Within* is a very practical and powerful book that, when read carefully and applied, is sure to help you reach your goals, and even beyond your goals to a level that you may not have thought possible.

I commend Swapna for putting together such a book, which highlights the various important aspects you have to consider and implement to achieve success. If you are looking to enhance your life by truly aligning your purpose and goals, this book will be invaluable to you.

I am confident that you will find *Your Journey Within* truly inspirational, and the insights taught by Swapna within this book are sure to help you create the life you deserve.

I strongly recommend that you read and implement the strategies and ideas put forth in this book to enhance your life.

Raymond Aaron
New York Times Bestselling Author

CHAPTER ONE

INTRODUCTION

Let me begin by congratulating you, my dearest reader, as you have made the important decision to pick this book up and read it. Very few people take action!

People often think about doing many great things in life, but very few actually act upon it. You are among the few who have chosen to be different, and are motivated to create the life you deserve.

Some people go through their entire life without having an aim or a goal. They simply wait for life to happen. When small children are asked what they would like to be when they grow up, the question is easy to answer. They have a list of things that they want to be or do in life. Right from being a doctor to an astronaut, everything is possible in their little world. We had these big dreams, and we believed in them when we were small.

But what happens after? You may say, "Life happens!"

What made me write this book?

When we are little, we are exposed to all kinds of negative and positive events. We are told what we can or cannot do, or how we should or should not behave and so forth. We are constantly influenced by our environment. The programming continually affects us and feeds into

1

our subconscious mind. It is this programming that we base our entire life upon. We then restrict ourselves. We start developing limiting beliefs, and convince ourselves that only certain things are possible. We start differentiating between what is a fantasy and what is realistic. Our reasoning mind takes over. Our beliefs are formed based on what we have experienced in life, or what has been taught to us by our parents, teachers, family and the society in which we live. Our environment has a huge impact on us.

Slowly we start to make decisions in life based on what we have been taught or experienced. We go from having unlimited potential to being realistic and conservative. We aim only for those things that we think we can achieve in life. Some of us do not even aim for anything because we have been told that we need to live within our means. We have either been taught this or we have witnessed this by seeing the way our parents lived all their lives. No, I am not saying that our parents were wrong. They were quite right in their own ways, as they were taught the same or they were programmed the same way. They did not know any other way and hence they did their best in raising their kids.

This is the main reason why I am writing this book. I want you as a reader to stop and think, what if you can change your life for the better? What if you were shown a path that is different and could bring you more desirable results so that you can now live a life you deserve? What if you could be able to once again start thinking about your dreams and start believing in them? What if you were told that it is never too late to start dreaming once again? This book will do just that. This book will bring out the unlimited potential that you have, and also show you the path you can follow to create the life you deserve.

But for that to happen, the most important factor is for you to be willing to change. You need to have the desire to do things differently in life.

If you need different results, you need to do things differently. You cannot expect to get different results by doing the same thing over and over again.

It all starts with you making a decision to change. Change is imperative. People are always afraid of change. But let me tell you, change is not always bad. In fact change is good. Change is needed for you to grow.

I understand that change can be very uncomfortable most of the time. But in order for you to achieve greatness or have a great life you need to get out of your comfort zone.

This is the number one reason why I decided to write this book. It is only after I decided to be uncomfortable that I started to grow. I now do things on a daily basis that I am totally uncomfortable with, but I know that it is the only way that I will be able to progress in life. To be honest, I never ever imagined that I would be writing a book in my lifetime. I was always a shy person and afraid of a lot of things. I had low self-esteem and had this weird misconception in my head that people always judged me for who I was. When I looked at all these successful men and women around me, I envied them. In my head I carried an image of myself as a person who lacked confidence and was timid.

But then one day I made the decision to change myself. I decided that I no longer liked the person I had become. I wanted to do something bigger in life, by which I would be remembered and make my family proud. I took courses, started learning with my mentors, and developed a passion for the field of personal development. This led me on my journey to self-development. I soon realized that if I can do it, anyone who has the motivation and the desire to improve their life can. I then decided I wanted to spread this powerful message to others who were eager but did not know the right path. Through this book,

I have now decided to help as many people as I can, on their journey to lead a happier and more meaningful life.

How will you benefit from this book?

My book is based on my experiences, and the principles and daily habits that I implement in my life. These are proven steps that, if taken in the right order and at appropriate times as mentioned in the book, will help you achieve your goals and dreams, just as I have been able to achieve mine. I have been fortunate to have esteemed mentors and coaches in my life, such as Raymond Aaron, Jack Canfield, Bob Proctor, Meir Ezra, who have taught me very important lessons, which I am now sharing with you through this book.

I believe success is a journey within us, and hence the title. I also strongly believe that we all have the power to create the life we desire. All we need is a path. In order to be successful on the outside, we need to first be successful on the inside. We need to develop ourselves and grow within, through constant learning and putting all the teachings into action. Just learning will get us nowhere. We need to put it into practice in our daily lives. Self-development is a continual process to see the results we desire.

It all starts with the right mindset.

As rightly said by Napoleon Hill in his book, *Think and Grow Rich*, "Whatever the mind can conceive and believe, it can achieve."

I believe it all starts with making the decision to create the life you desire. First you have to decide, believe, plan, and then act upon it. There are many factors to consider during this process, and we will be discussing those in the following chapters that will lead to your path to success.

Who is this book for?

This book is for people like you, who have decided to commit to improvement in life and are willing to take the steps needed to achieve the life they deserve. Remember it is a journey, "your journey within," that you will be going through as you put into practice all the action steps outlined in this book. Let me warn you though; it is not for the weak. It is not always a bed of roses. There are times you will be put to test. Certain times you may experience failure or might be tempted to give up, but only those who have a strong will and are capable of handling disappointments will survive this entire journey. The stronger your desire, the more your chances to succeed. Your determination and willpower will get you to your goals.

**"Every Failure Brings With It
The Seed Of An Equivalent Success"
- Think and Grow Rich**

Why should you read this book?

Many of the teachings of my mentors will be reflected constantly throughout this book. Hence I can confidently say that all the material and the chapters in this book, if read carefully and followed consistently, will lead you to your path to success. Like I said before, this is your journey that you are embarking upon, and I wish you my dear friend all the very best! I sincerely want you to create the life you desire and deserve. Just read through the chapters, follow the principles, understand the concepts, believe in the possibilities, take proper actions, and you will be on your way to success!

CHAPTER 2

DARE TO DREAM

"I HAVE A DREAM"- Martin Luther King Jr.

The historic speech "I have a dream," delivered by American civil rights activist Martin Luther King Jr. during the March on Washington for Jobs and Freedom on August 28, 1963, has gone down in history and was the hallmark of the civil rights movement.

Martin Luther King Jr. was extremely clear in what he wanted, and he had the courage and determination to go for it.

Do you have a dream?

I am strongly suggesting that you need to have a dream. Dreams are important, as they give you a sense of direction in life. They motivate, inspire, improve and help you in achieving any goal that you want to achieve. All achievements, whether big or small, start by having dreams and following them. Dreams give a meaning to your life. You start living a life with a purpose. When you decide on your dreams you become alive and start experiencing life in a much deeper sense. When you define your dreams you set an intention and act upon it. As it is rightly said, by James Redfield, "where your intention is your attention grows." Defining your dreams makes you aware of the unlimited potential you have. What is within you is greater than any external circumstances.

Why are people afraid to have a dream?

If having dreams is so important then why don't we all have them? Why is it so difficult for us to answer the question "What is it that I really want in life?"

The vast majority of people have trouble describing and deciding on their dreams because they are afraid. There is a fear of being ridiculed. People are afraid of being judged by others. They have the belief that they need to fit within the society. They feel that they have to think like everyone else, and that if they think or act differently they will not be accepted within the community. Hence they just drown in the sea of sameness. They are afraid of being different. All their lives they just go with the masses.

There is a great quote that I love and live by, which states,
"Why fit in when you were born to stand out?"- Dr. Seuss.

Learn to be different. Practice dream-building.

Do not let others steal your dreams

Do not let people discourage you from pursuing your dreams. I have been often asked if it wise to share our dreams with other people. My answer to this question is yes! You should share your dreams with others. The reason I am saying this is because once you put your dream out there, there may be others who share similar interests and have common goals. These people may in fact encourage you and help you in building your dreams and achieving them.

If Martin Luther King Jr. hadn't shared his dream with the entire nation, we would have seen a different history. If Gandhi hadn't shared his dream and vision about independence for India, the country would still be under British rule.

There are many thought leaders and mentors who are not in favor of sharing dreams, but I strongly believe that the more you talk to people about your dreams the stronger they become, and the chances of others supporting your dreams increase.

Why is it important to have a dream?

One important lesson you need to learn is, don't live someone else's dream. Since childhood we have been told what we have to do or what we should be doing. This leads to us losing touch with our wishes and needs. We have been told what school to go to, what profession to choose, sometimes even who is a suitable life partner. Eventually we become numb to our wants and desires. We try so hard to be sensible that we learn to suppress our real feelings. We learn to act based on the expectations of our parents and society, just to get their approval.

The other reason why people do not have dreams is due to their self-limiting beliefs. Pay attention to your limiting beliefs. Pay attention to your thoughts. You may have been conditioned to believe you have very limited potential and can only achieve so much in life. You may have been told not to aim for the sky. With constant programming like this all your life, it is only natural that you stop dreaming! You start doubting yourself. You become unsure of your capabilities. You start harboring thoughts such as, who am I? Who am I to be able to think of dreaming big? With all the limited resources that I have, what right do I have to be able to set big goals in life?

The other big limiting belief is age. Maybe I am too young or too old to start dreaming about the things that I want to do in life. Self-doubt is the number one killer of your dreams. Let me tell you something, age has nothing to do with what your dreams are. These self-limiting beliefs sabotage your progress in life. The only way you can get rid of these limits is by changing your thoughts.

"Thoughts become things" - Napoleon Hill

Your thoughts are so powerful that they can even move mountains. It all depends on how badly you want your dream. If you have a burning desire, nothing can stop you from achieving it. Once you have your dreams defined, your thoughts get aligned to them. All you need to do is start thinking of how you can possess what you desire and take the needed action in that direction. In your mind you have to know that you can have anything that you desire, then the universe starts aligning in such a way that you ultimately get what you want. It all starts with the first step of deciding your dreams and then believing in them. Once this foundation is built, then you need to start thinking of the ways you can achieve what you long for.

What is your dream?

Let me start you off by asking these few questions:

1. What is your dream?
2. What are your burning desires?
3. What is that you really want?
4. What kind of life would you like to live?
5.What would you love to be, do, create, express, experience?

Once you have the answers to these questions, I encourage you to start thinking about and writing down your dreams. The reason you need to write them down is that once you have them in black and white they become real. It has been proven that if you have something written down it gets lodged in your subconscious mind, and once that happens you can manifest it in life. You might have a very strong single dream, or you might have a dream in every area of your life. But it is extremely important for you to write them down.

How can you turn your dreams into reality?

As Mary Morrissey states, "Dreams speak to us in 2 ways, through longing and through discontent." Pay attention to what you long for in life. Pay close attention to your discontent. Listen to your inner voice. This will help you writing down your dreams. Do not think realistically. Do not try and reason out your dreams. Initially just put down anything that you want without having to think of the 'how.' It is the 'what' that is important right now; the 'how' will show up.

There is a great exercise by Jack Canfield, in his book *The Success Principles,* where asks the reader to make an "I want list." This is a powerful exercise, and I want you to do it. The exercise will help you begin to clarify what you truly want in life.

In this exercise, make a list of 30 things you want to do, 30 things you want to have, and 30 things you want to be before you die. This is a great way to start your thought process.

So set aside all the pre-conceived ideas you had up until now about yourself. Put away all your self-doubt and limiting beliefs and start listing your dreams.

By now you should have a pretty clear picture of what your dream looks like. You should be able to identify what is it that you really want, and you should have written it down.

The next step is to start believing in your dreams. Until and unless you have the faith in your dreams, and in yourself, you cannot achieve anything.

"Faith is the only known antidote for failure." – Napoleon Hill

Once you have the faith, you can force all the negative emotions and thoughts out of your mind. You can now control your mind the way you want it to think, and attain great heights.

Are you worthy of your dream?
Is your dream worthy of you?

Now that you have your dream, there are two very important factors that you need to consider before you start planning your action steps. The first one is "Are you worthy of your dream?" The second question, which is more important, is "Is your dream worthy of you?" This question means you have to be absolutely sure that this dream is right for you. Your dreams are unique to you. You have to know that you are worthy of them. You need to test your dream. Just because an idea comes up does not mean it is right for you.

Believing in your dream

You need the conviction that this is really what you want, and then go for it. The best way to know is to consider how you feel about your dream when you think or read about it. Does it energize you? Does it make you come alive? Does it fill you with immense happiness just thinking about it? Do you feel contained or constricted? Does it make you want to jump with joy or does it pull you down? These are extremely important questions you need to ask yourself before you make a final decision about your dream.

Although your dream is extremely personal, does it also benefit others in some way? Let me explain.

How does your dream benefit others?

People have certain dreams about contributing in some way to their society or community. Does your dream do good for others? Do you feel the joy and satisfaction of serving others through your dream? It could be a direct or indirect service. You may be physically contributing towards the good of others or simply living a dream that inspires and motivates others to do the same. Your dreams could be the source of inspiration for others who want to achieve something in life but are simply afraid to take the first step.

By living your dream you could be setting an example to thousands around you who need encouragement and motivation to live the life they desire.

Our mind always thinks in images. It creates good or bad images depending on how we cultivate our thoughts. The best way to build your dream is by thinking in pictures. You can find photographs or pictures of things you want in life, the places you want to visit, or the lifestyle you wish to have. This will help you focus on what you really want, and help you achieve your goals faster. I sincerely urge you to stop settling for less than what you want, and start building your dreams!

EXERCISE 1 - DECIDING ON YOUR DREAM

If time, money, age, education, gender were not an issue, list 10 things you would really want to do, be or have.

1. _____

2. _____

3. _____

4. _____

5. _____

6. _____

7. _____

8. _____

9. _____

10._____

Notes:

_____

_____

_____

_____

_____

_____

_____

_____

_____

_____

_____

_____

_____

_____

Notes:

_____

_____

_____

_____

_____

_____

_____

_____

_____

_____

_____

_____

_____

_____

Notes:

_____

_____

_____

_____

_____

_____

_____

_____

_____

_____

_____

_____

_____

_____

Notes:

_____

_____

_____

_____

_____

_____

_____

_____

_____

_____

_____

_____

_____

_____

_____

CHAPTER 3

DEFINING YOUR PURPOSE

The Purpose Of Our Lives Is To Be Happy
- Dalai Lama

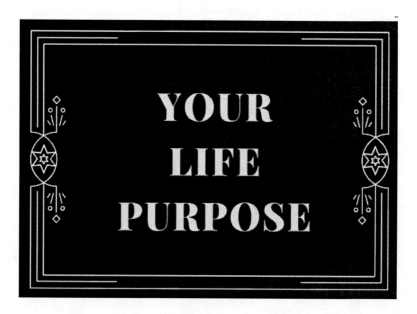

What is a life purpose?

Now that you have a dream that is precious to you, it is extremely important for you to discover what makes you happy. You have been given this gift called life and you need to figure out the meaning of this gift, and how you can give it to others.

Until now you may have lived, but do you think just living is enough? Or does living a life full of purpose and reason add value and meaning to your life?

Why is it important to have a life purpose?

I wanted to discover my purpose because wanted to find out what I was put on this earth to do. I wanted to contribute to this planet in a way that would bring me peace and joy. I wanted to give in such a way that it would not only benefit others but also give me satisfaction and containment. Let me tell you, it was not easy at the beginning to find my life purpose. It may seem complicated to you as well at first, but once you learn the correct way you can figure it out too.

My Life Purpose is to inspire and empower people to create the life they desire and deserve through my knowledge and creativity so that they in turn help others live a life of their highest purpose.

How can you define your purpose?

Here are some questions that will help you in discovering your Life Purpose:

1. Why are you here?
2. Why are you living?
3. Why are you doing what you are doing?
4. What were you put on this earth to do?
5. What are you passionate about?

One way to discover your purpose is by identifying what you are passionate about. What is it that, if given a chance, you can endlessly talk about without getting tired? What is it that brings you immense joy and a sense of fulfillment? Each and every one of us do has certain ideas that when expressed bring happiness in our lives. Some of us are able to identify them easily, while for some it takes a lot of probing and soul searching to be able to recognize them. Either way, once you know what it is that makes you come alive you have discovered your purpose.

You need to write down your life purpose. It is not something you decide on but it is something you need to discover.

"The two most important days of your life are the day you were born, and the day your find out why." - Mark Twain

Your life purpose is a statement that reflects your burning desire, your why and your what. Your life purpose is very unique to you. You need to have a clear purpose in life. Your life purpose should reflect your core values, your unique abilities and the qualities you possess. Bob Proctor says, "Your purpose is like your life compass that guides you through every step of your life." As explained by Jack Canfield, it is like the GPS (global positioning device) in your car that takes you to where you want to go.

It gives you direction and shows you the way. All you need to do is know where you are and where you want to go. It indicates to you immediately if you are off course and helps you to get back on track. Your purpose should bring you joy. Once you discover your purpose you can plan your action steps and activities around it.

"Until thought is linked with purpose there is no intelligent accomplishment"- James Allen

If you have no purpose in life you will easily fall prey to worries, fears, failures, doubts and self-pity. Without a life purpose it is very easy to get sidetracked in life's journey. It is very easy to get strayed from your path and your goals. When you know your purpose you will automatically do things that are aligned with your purpose. It helps you to make decisions faster. Everything seems to fall in place. You will only be doing those things that you love to do, doing only what you are good at, and accomplishing what is important to you.

Exercise to help you define your purpose

There are quite a few different exercises that all the great mentors and teachers have described in different books to identify life purpose. The one I like the best is the one in the book The Success Principles by Jack Canfield. There are three steps in this exercise. The first step is to list two of your unique qualities. The second step is to list two ways you enjoy expressing these qualities when interacting with others. The third step is to describe what a perfect world looks like to you.

Let's take my life purpose for example:

1. My two unique qualities - knowledge and creativity
2. Two ways of expressing these qualities - inspire and empower
3. My description of a perfect world - where people are creating the life they deserve and in turn helping others to live a life of purpose

Putting it all together, my Life Purpose is "to inspire and empower people to create a life they deserve, through my knowledge and creativity, so that they in turn help others live a life of purpose." I also feel extremely aligned with my purpose, as I am writing this book and sharing my knowledge with you so I can inspire and empower you to create the life you desire and deserve. I sincerely hope that after reading this book you will be able to do the same for other people so that they in turn live a purposeful and meaningful life.

There are other different tools that you can use to identify and discover your life purpose, such as meditation, visualization, and guided imagery. In order for you to have your life purpose come to you, you need to have a calm mind. Meditation or guided meditation is the best way to calm your mind when you seek answers.

"Calmness of mind is one of the beautiful jewels of wisdom"-
As a Man Thinketh **by James Allen**

If your mind is crowded with thoughts, you may on many occasions miss the one idea that could have been life changing for you. When your mind is calm, you are able to see all the opportunities that come your way. You feel more powerful and in control. You are able to make decisions wisely. You are even able to share your wisdom with others so that they in turn can be in better control of their lives.

Different tools you can use to identify your life purpose

The other powerful tool to discover your purpose is visualization. Through this technique you are able to clearly visualize the process and the outcomes. Visualization helps you create images through which you can gain clarity on your purpose. When you visualize, you are seeing events already happen. You are seeing images of your accomplishments. This process helps you analyze your feelings towards the events, and that in turn will help you in clarifying your purpose.

How is life purpose different than life mission?

I believe that your life purpose guides you and your mission drives you. They are very closely connected. Your mission could be a part of your life purpose. My life mission is to be a great inspiration, and this complements my life purpose, which is to inspire and motivate. Different mentors and gurus may have different opinions about this, but this is how I have interpreted the two.

My powerful mentor, Raymond Aaron, who I respect and love a lot, taught me the concept of *Be, Do, Have*. He has taught me the process of identifying my life missions. He says that vast majority of people get it backwards, but the correct order in achieving your goals and fulfilling your life missions is to first be that person you want to be, and then do what that person would do, in order to have what you want. For example, one of my life missions is to be a great inspiration to people both known and unknown to me. But for me to accomplish this life mission I need to have an image of myself in my head, that I am a true inspiration to thousands. Only then will I be able to complete my life mission. I need to change myself first, before I can go around influencing and changing other people. Once I am thoroughly convinced that I have the capacity and the power to bring about the change in society, I will be able to do something about it, which will then get me the desired outcome

EXERCISE 2 - DISCOVERING YOUR LIFE PURPOSE

A. LIST 3 activities that you absolutely love to do

e.g. reading, writing, teaching, inspiring, motivating etc.

1. _____

2. _____

3. _____

B. WRITE DOWN YOUR "WHY" (THE COMPELLING REASON BEHIND YOUR ACTIONS)

e.g. your love for animals, your love for your family, your love for the society in which you live, your love for your country etc.

_____

_____

_____

_____

_____

C. WRITE DOWN YOUR LIFE PURPOSE STATEMENT

e.g. My Life purpose is : "To inspire and empower people to create a life they deserve through my knowledge and creativity so that they in turn help others live a life of their highest purpose."

_____

_____

_____

_____

Notes:

_____

_____

_____

_____

_____

_____

_____

_____

_____

_____

_____

_____

_____

_____

Notes:

_____

_____

_____

_____

_____

_____

_____

_____

_____

_____

_____

_____

_____

_____

Notes:

_____

_____

_____

_____

_____

_____

_____

_____

_____

_____

_____

_____

_____

_____

_____

CHAPTER 4

CLARIFYING YOUR VISION

"Follow your passion and success will follow you"
- Arthur Buddhold

Are you living a life full of passion and purpose?
Are you truly passionate about what you are doing on a daily basis?
Do you want to find direction in life? Find your passion and you will find your direction.

When you wake up in the morning, what are the first thoughts that come to your mind? These thoughts will indicate if you are living a life of purpose and passion.

How do you feel when the weekend comes to an end? On Monday mornings do you feel dragged down or are you energized to start your day and your week? The answers to these questions will guide you in the right direction. They will help you discover your purpose in life.

What is it that you really want?

When you are passionate about certain things in life, no matter what obstacles come your way you will have the strength to face all odds and go for that passion, that dream you have built. That is your real "why." Hence it is extremely important to have a dream, a life purpose, a passion and a vision of your ideal life.

You need to define your vision for your ideal life. A life that is extraordinary and full of possibilities. You need to clarify this vision. Make it so clear that your fears become irrelevant. Vision is the big picture of what you want your life to look like. Hold on to your vision! It does not matter if other people are unable to see your vision, or if they do not believe in your vision, because if the vision is clear in your mind and you are committed to it nothing can stop you from turning it into reality.

Create a vision that makes you jump out of bed every morning. You may not know what your vision is in the beginning, or you may only have a vague idea about it. This is alright. It is a process that involves a lot of thinking and feeling.

You can start yourself by asking questions such as "What do I want my life to look like?"

Is there someone such as a speaker, a celebrity, a prominent figure or a hero you look up to? How would it feel to live a life like they do? Do you envy someone and wish you had all that they have? What would your ideal day look like? Do you have a free day? A day where you can do what you want when you want, or not do anything at all? Do you wish you had such days? Just wishing is not going to get you anywhere. You need to act upon it, and the way to start that is by defining your dream, discovering your life purpose, identifying your passion and clarifying your vision.

How far are you willing to go to get it in life?

Your vision has to be clear to you, in a way that you can experience it. Put your feelings into it. When you define your vision, you need to be aware of how you feel about it. You have to include all five senses in order to clarify your vision. You need to see clearly, hear the sounds that you may hear when you are living your vision, smell that you would smell in your vision, touch and feel the things that are included in your vision, and taste the sensations that you would taste.

Creating images and vision board

One way to create your vision is by using a vision board. A vision board is a very powerful tool with which you can capture your dreams and your longings. It is a board on which you can paste pictures of your dreams, big or small. You can put up pictures of the things that you want in life, and what your life would look like. You need to put dates on each of your goals. A vision without a plan is merely a dream. Creating this vision board and looking at it every day helps you to clarify, concentrate and maintain focus on the things that you desire, and the life you want to create for yourself. The theory behind creating a vision board is that it has been proven time and time again that what we focus on grows. If you want good in your life, you need to focus on the good. Put all your attention on something and it expands.

Clarifying your vision through guided visualization, meditation and affirmations

I have mentioned in the previous chapters the power of visualization. Visualization is the most powerful mind exercise. This technique is used by many Olympic athletes. To create your vision board you must learn to visualize and then believe in yourself. You have to put emotions in your visualization. When you visualize your dreams and goals, the more energy and emotion you put in the better the ultimate result will be.

You have to make a commitment to yourself. Sometimes this can be scary. You may have to give up something to gain something. You may have to give up certain habits, change certain behavioural patterns, and most importantly change the way you think. Your thoughts are very critical in deciding your success or failure in life. You may have to make certain choices differently than you have been so far. If you need to get different results you should be willing to act differently. Always keep the end game in mind. Do whatever it takes to get you to your end goal. As described in Roman mythology, the ruler who burned his boats after conquering the territory, similarly "Burn your boats" so that you do not have the option of failing.

One of Jack Canfield's success principles states, "See what you want, get what you see." In this principle he emphasizes the importance of visualization. He defines visualization as " the act of creating compelling and vivid pictures in your mind."

Further he explains the effects of visualization. He states that this process activates the creative powers of your subconscious mind, focuses your brain by programming the reticular activating system to create awareness of the resources available and through the 'Law of Attraction' attracts to you the people, resources and opportunities you need to achieve your goals and fulfill your dreams.

Along with visualization it is also very important to affirm for yourself daily. Affirmations help purify our thoughts and restructure the dynamic of our brains so that we truly begin to think nothing is impossible. Positive affirmations help you raise your internal vibrations and strengthen your beliefs. Affirmations are very effective when made in the present tense such as "I am so happy and grateful now that I..." (you can write down a goal that you have)

An extremely powerful affirmation is a personal daily affirmation that starts with

"I am..." Examples:
"I am happy"
"I am worthy of my dreams"
"I am powerful"
"I am on my way to creating great wealth"

Your vision helps you focus on your dream. It helps you gain clarity of the life you desire and deserve. The more clear you are about what you want, the more likely it is that you will achieve it.

Do not be like the vast majority of people out there who can see but do not have a vision.

Instead create a vision, which reflects your insight and opens up the door to your soul.

**"Action without vision is only passing time,
Vision without action is merely day dreaming,
But vision with action can change the world"
- Nelson Mandela**

The next step to take towards creating the life you deserve is to set goals.

So far you have a dream, you know your life purpose, you are aware of what it is that you are passionate about, you have created a vision of your ideal life. Now you need to set goals so that you can plan and take action. Goals are dreams with a deadline.

In the next chapter I will be discussing everything about goal setting. You will learn the importance of having goals, the correct and effective method of goal setting, having goals in different areas of your life - health, finance, relationships, work and career, business, personal - and the importance of visualizing your goals and focusing on achieving them.

**"Vision without execution is delusion"
- Thomas Edison**

EXERCISE 3 - CLARIFY YOUR VISION

WRITE DOWN YOUR VISION FOR DIFFERENT AREAS OF YOUR LIFE e.g. finance, career, relationships etc.

IF MY LIFE WAS IDEAL, MY WORLD WOULD LOOK LIKE THIS...

MY CLEAR AND IDEAL VISION FOR -

1. FINANCE: (ideal annual income, monthly cash flow, retirement funds etc.)

_____

_____

_____

2. CAREER: (job, business etc.)

_____

_____

_____

3. HEALTH: (your ideal body weight, your exercise routine, your eating habits etc.)

_____

_____

_____

4. RELATIONSHIPS: (with family, your spouse, your friends, your colleagues etc.)

_____
_____
_____

5. PERSONAL: (hobbies you may have, going to back to school, taking spiritual lessons, play an instrument etc.)

_____
_____
_____

6. RECREATION: (travel, vacations, how do you utilize your free time etc.)

_____
_____
_____

7. COMMUNITY : (charity, volunteering, philanthropy etc.)

_____
_____
_____

Notes:

_____

_____

_____

_____

_____

_____

_____

_____

_____

_____

_____

_____

_____

_____

Notes:

_____

_____

_____

_____

_____

_____

_____

_____

_____

_____

_____

_____

_____

_____

Notes:

_____

_____

_____

_____

_____

_____

_____

_____

_____

_____

_____

_____

_____

_____

CHAPTER 5

IDENTIFYING YOUR GOALS

A dream is just a dream. A goal is a dream with a plan and a deadline - Harvey Mackey

The importance of having goals

What is the first thing that comes to your mind when you hear the word *goals*?

Is it a deadline? Is it the pressure to achieve them? Is it things that you have to do? Is it the pathway to success or is it the joy you will experience after achieving the goals?

Why do people not set goals?

The majority of people have heard about goals, and have set goals for themselves. But the difficulty is to follow through with those goals. So many times in the past they have not been met, and hence they have come to a point where they do not believe in goal setting anymore. I was in this exact situation a few years ago. I was setting some goals for January 1 of each year, also called New Year's resolutions, but due to the incorrect rules that I followed to set the goals up, and a lack of follow-up, I have given up on them.

If you are in the same situation, believe me, you're not alone. There are people who let go of their New Year's resolutions before noon on January 2!!!

I believe the main reason why people are not achieving their goals is that they do not know how to set them up correctly, and they do not use a system to follow through to see if they have met their goals.

The importance of goal setting

Having said that, it is important to note that setting up any type of goal is better than setting up no goal at all.

Setting clear, measurable goals

Here are a few rules that you should follow if you want to set up effective and achievable goals:

1. Keep it simple: The first rule of goal setting is it has to be simple, in terms of the language. It has to be clear to you as to what exactly it means, and how you will know that it has been achieved. Keeping it simple also makes it clear in your mind, so that the steps that you need to take to achieve the goal also can be simplified.

2. Keep it achievable: This is one of the major causes of goal achievement failures. Your goals may be so vast and out of reach for you that they may be great to achieve and have, but you may have never done anything like that before. For example, if you have never run a marathon before, setting a goal to run a marathon in the next 6 months may not be the goal that you should start with.
How about running a 5k in the next 3 - 6 months?

There are two reasons why this is very crucial:

A. It is more real to you, and hence your belief in it is higher and you increase your chances of achieving it.

B. Once you start achieving smaller goals, your confidence in your ability to achieve goals goes up, and you can scale up from that level. It therefore becomes a self-fulfilling prophecy.

If you find yourself always not able to meet a goal, try lowering the gradient.

3. Have a realistic timeframe: You may have a goal and the only reason that you are not achieving that goal is because the goal has a time-frame that is not realistic.

If you think about it, this might be the only factor why you're not achieving your goal! In the previous example of running a marathon, perhaps only the time-frame is incorrect, and if you give it enough time the goal is quite possible!

4. Monitor your goals after your deadline: How often do you monitor your goals to check if you are on track? Do you think having a look at your goals on a daily basis will make a difference? I have seen a lot of people write goals and forget where they have written them. Once the goal is set, it is very critical for you to go back to that goal each and every day, review it, and try to come up with very small steps that you can take towards attainment of it.

5. Modify your goals: This may be something unusual for you, but let me explain. If you have a goal that you have set for yourself, and you have been trying to achieve it for a very long time but have been unsuccessful, the next best thing is to modify it by breaking it down. The reason this is important is that you have now increased the chances of reaching that goal. Once you have reached it, you may decide to go back to the original goal that you have set up.

6. Delegate Delegate Delegate! This is one aspect of goal setting that I had a lot of trouble with. I always thought that nobody could do it better than me. I do not have the funds to ask someone to do it for me. Where can I find people to do it for me? Will they do it according to what I want?

Statements and questions like these kept me away from delegating my tasks, and slowed down my progress. However, since I have learned the secret and started to apply on a lower gradient, I began to see huge designs in my life and my business.

Usually, the first question that comes to mind is "How can I hire someone if I don't have the money?" Let me help you with that. The compensation that you give someone in order to get your task done does not always need to be monetary. If you are an expert in a certain field, you can always offer your services in return for the service that you're looking for. Following Jack Canfield's principle of asking, I am sure that you can find someone that offers exactly what you are looking for.

My mentor Raymond Aaron taught me this principle, and now I am always on the lookout for people that can do things that I'm not good at.

This is a total win-win because you get to do what you're good at and delegate the things that you're not good at.

The most effective way to set goals

In his book *Double Your Income Doing What You Love*, Raymond Aaron describes a very powerful strategy to set up, achieve and reach all your goals. His system of goal setting is called *MAINLY*.

The main concept of his system of setting goals is that you need to set up three levels for each goal. The first level is the *minimum* level that you think you can achieve. The second is the *target*, which is the level you really want to reach. The third is *outrageous*, which is a level you would love to reach but which seems impossible at this time.

The most amazing thing about setting up your goals with this technique is that you never fail. The minimum that you achieve is the minimum that you have set for yourself, but you also may achieve something that you have set up as an outstanding goal. Using this method safeguards you from failing to achieve your goals.

In his book, Raymond goes into much more detail about setting the goals correctly, as well as how to monitor them on a monthly basis.

Having goals in different areas of your life - health, finance, relationships, work and career, business, personal

Once you understand the correct way of setting goals and start setting it up for yourself, I would encourage you to set up goals in all the areas of your life.

The principle of goal setting remains the same for all the areas of life, but you may have to modify them according to your business or your workplace. The reason being, you might be working in a team, and having the entire team aligned with your goals is a critical component of success.

It is very important to involve your coworkers or team in your goal setting, so you can get the maximum leverage from them. In addition to that, by teaching this correct way of setting goals, you are providing a lot of value to your team as they can go ahead and use these principles to set up goals in their own personal lives.

The importance of visualizing your goals

Now that you have your goals written down in the correct manner, I am so happy for you, as now comes the exciting step.

I would encourage you to start visualizing these goals that you have put down on paper as already complete!

Yes, you do have to visualize that the goals are already complete.

This is very important for the goal attainment process because the mind cannot conceive the difference between reality and fantasy. The gap that exists between the reality and vividly imagined events now starts to create a structural tension between the two in your mind.

This visualization exercise is so powerful that it could give you a sense of achievement even before you actually have the thing in your possession. The visualization exercise can be done in 5 to 10 minutes every day, just before going to sleep and first thing when you wake up in the morning. It reinforces your goals, and it automatically channelizes you to do the things that are necessary to achieve your goals.

When you're visualizing, pay careful attention to the feelings that you're experiencing, the smells that you may be experiencing, the sounds that you may hear around you, the people that surround you, the ambiance around at that time, etc. In other words, the more life you can put in your goals when you're doing the visualization, the more real you can make it seem, the more it will push you towards doing the things that you need to do to achieve that goal.

When you're visualizing your goals, you may be able to see some images in your mind about the goals that you have set up. However, for some of you, it may not be very easy to do so. And that's where the importance of the vision board comes into play. Your vision board is created and placed somewhere you see it on a regular basis. Now you can cut out images, print images, buy posters and whatever else you need to do to get your goals in the form of images. All these pictures and cutouts can go on your vision board which you can use during this exercise.

You can also get a little more creative, and use Photoshop to have your picture with a background of where you want to travel, or in front of a car that you want to own, or have your family picture in front of the house that you want to buy. Do you think doing things like this will make it easier for you to visualize? Of course it will.

Some people, on the other hand, can actually see their goals as already achieved, can hear them, feel them, and also visualize it as a video. Though it might seem as if these people are achieving their goals much faster, that's not reality. For the purpose of goal setting and visualization exercise any method that is outlined above will work the same. The main thing is to do it on a consistent basis twice a day for you to see amazing results.

How about actually experiencing your goals achieved?

This is the ultimate way of reinforcing your goal setting technique. Once you have a clearly defined goal, I would encourage you to go ahead and get a taste of how it will feel once the goal is actually achieved.

For example, if your goal is to purchase a specific car, can you go to a car dealership and take a test drive? If you have a specific type of house that you want to buy, can you call your realtor and arrange to have a look at a few houses to make it easy for you to visualize your goals?

Now that you have your goals clearly defined, written and have started the process of visualization, you are ahead of most people who do not even have the right method to set up the goals.

Once you start the process of daily visualizing and clarifying your goals, the only things that could discourage you are the obstacles that will pop up on your pathway to achieving your goals. These obstacles are also known as road blocks, and I am going to teach you how to overcome your roadblocks in the next chapter.

Worrying is simply negative goal setting - Zig Ziglar

EXERCISE 4 - GOALS SETTING

SET : S = SPECIFIC (what)

M = MEASURABLE (how much)

T = TIME PERIOD (by when)

SET GOALS IN THE FOLLOWING AREAS OF YOUR LIFE :
(use your vision exercise to set goals)

A.   FINANCIAL GOALS -
_____
_____
_____

B. CAREER GOALS -
_____
_____
_____

C. HEALTH GOALS -
_____
_____
_____

D. RELATIONSHIP GOALS -
_____
_____
_____

E. RECREATIONAL GOALS -

_____
_____
_____

F. PERSONAL GOALS -

_____
_____
_____

G. CONTRIBUTION GOALS -

_____
_____
_____

WRITE DOWN ONE MAJOR BREAKTHROUGH GOAL THAT YOU WILL ACHIEVE THIS MONTH

_____
_____
_____
_____

WRITE DOWN THE AFFIRMATION FOR THE BREAKTHROUGH GOAL - "I am so happy and grateful now that,

_____
_____
_____
_____
_____

Your Journey Within

Notes:

_____

_____

_____

_____

_____

_____

_____

_____

_____

_____

_____

_____

_____

Notes:

_____

_____

_____

_____

_____

_____

_____

_____

_____

_____

_____

_____

_____

_____

Notes:

_____

_____

_____

_____

_____

_____

_____

_____

_____

_____

_____

_____

_____

_____

_____

Notes:

_____

_____

_____

_____

_____

_____

_____

_____

_____

_____

_____

_____

_____

_____

_____

CHAPTER 6

CLEARING YOUR ROADBLOCKS

*Obstacles are those frightful things you see when you take
your eyes off your goal
- Henry Ford*

What are roadblocks?

Roadblocks are the interruptions you encounter when trying to achieve a goal in life.

They are the obstacles that you come across when you get distracted from your life purpose. You will face a lot of hurdles in life that you will have to overcome in order to create the life you deserve. When you lose your focus of achieving success, you hit all kinds of roadblocks.

Different types of roadblocks

Roadblocks can be internal or external. They can be physical blocks, mental blocks or emotional blocks. Sometimes these roadblocks can also be induced by other people or the environment you live in.

It is not what I say to you that matters, but it is what you say to yourself that makes a difference. These are your thoughts! Your thoughts could be the number one roadblock for you if you do not train them. If you want positive results you need to think positive. You also need to take full responsibility for your thoughts, actions and behaviours. You have to stop complaining, blaming and making excuses. All these contribute to the slowing down of your progress, so you need to eliminate these negative habits from your life. If you want to be successful you have to take full responsibility for everything that you experience in life.

The most effective way is to apply Jack Canfield's Success Principle where he teaches the formula: E + R = O   (Event + Response = Outcome)

This concept is very powerful. It means that for every outcome that you experience or come across in life, be it success, failure, riches, poverty, health or illness, joy or frustration, is the result of the way you have responded to an event or events that have happened in your life. You are entirely responsible for all that has happened in your life so far, and all that you will be creating in the future. You have the ability to choose and create the life you desire. You have the choice of making good or bad decisions. It is entirely in your hands how you want to shape your future. Even if you have made the wrong decisions in the past, you now have the opportunity to correct your past mistakes and create a better life for yourself.

If you are not happy with the outcome that you have received so far, you need to change your response. You need to change your thinking, change your communication, change the images you hold in your mind, the change your faulty behavioural patterns. You have the power to change all that to create the life you deserve.

Getting out of your comfort zone

The vast majority of people often blame external circumstances or situations for their failures. They blame the weather, the economy, the lack of education, the lack of money, their parents, their teachers, their society and even their fate for all the negative outcomes in their lives. I agree that these factors do exist, that they probably play a major role in people's lives, but it depends on how they are dealt with. There are many people out there who, despite having all these limiting factors, are extremely successful. The only reason why they have achieved great wealth, health and prosperity is because they are aware of how to control the outcomes by responding in a favourable manner. They overcame these so-called limiting factors or roadblocks by changing their thoughts, behaviours and actions. They take 100% responsibility for their actions and behaviours. Successful people have given up the bad habit of blaming someone or something for their failure. They are also aware that there is absolutely no use complaining about anything to anybody. Most of the time you are complaining to the wrong person, who can do nothing about it anyway. So if you find yourself in a situation you don't like, either find ways to make it better yourself or get out of it.

At this point my question to you is, do you create everything that happens in your life or do you allow everything that happens to you? You need to reflect on this question as it is a key question, which will probably give you the answer why you are not living the life you desire. When you take full control of your life it becomes easier. You now have the ability to choose. Try replacing your vocabulary from "I have to" to "I choose to." When you say "I choose to" it puts you in control. You are now in a position to choose either to accept or reject any idea that comes your way. Your thoughts start to align with your purpose and you achieve success.

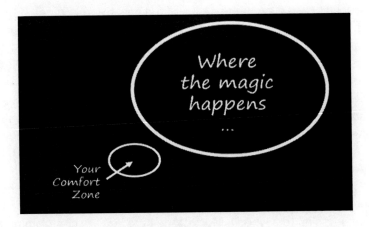

Identifying your roadblocks and fears

Successful people know how to overcome their emotional roadblocks. They get rid of their limiting self-beliefs and their fears. They face their fears and take steps to create their desired outcomes. They get out of their comfort zones to take the necessary actions in the direction of their dreams. Sometimes you have to take risks to be able to succeed. But if you are willing to take full responsibility for all that you will get, you will be successful in the true sense. You have to get rid of the victim mentality. You need to ask yourself constantly, "What have I done to create this in my life?"

Start paying attention to your thoughts, behaviours, actions, habits and self-talk. You may be holding certain images in your mind that were formed due to previous childhood programming, and because of this you may be acting or doing certain things that are impacting your life negatively. Try and recognize these thought patterns and behaviours, and either get rid of them or change them for the better. Dig deeper and bring them to the surface to alter them for a successful life.

"You become like the five people you spend the most time with" - Jim Rohn

Association is the key to success

Associate and surround yourself with positive, like-minded individuals. Stay away from toxic people. Toxic people are those who drain your energy levels. They seldom have anything uplifting to say, and they are usually dragging you down. These are the external roadblocks in your path to create the life you deserve. They are the doubters, the unsuccessful and broke people.

These people show lack of confidence in you, and induce negativity in your life. These people are the ones who, even by mentioning their names, make you feel constricted and stressed. These are the people in your life who can bring tension, stress and chaos to your day, just by a phone call or email, or for that matter any form of communication. These are what Jack Canfield calls the "dream stealers."

They are constantly reminding you of what is not possible, how difficult it is or how stressful life can be. If you have such people in your life you either need to get rid of them or decrease your association with them. Maybe you cannot completely eliminate them from your life, especially if they are family, but you can surely decide for yourself how much time you want to spend with them.

"Surround yourself with only people who are going to lift you higher"
- Oprah Winfrey

Surround yourself with those who make you happy. Listen to positive people and ignore negative people. People that doubt, judge and disrespect you are not worth your time and effort. Surround yourself with positive people who are going to push you towards greatness. Positive people do not put others down. Be among people who support you, encourage you, believe in you and bring out the best in you. Associate with like-minded individuals who share the same passion as you, who have common goals and who dream as big as you. These people will help you create the life you desire as they may share the same vision as you do. Be friends with people who take pride and joy in knowing you, and who accept you for who you are.

These are the people who see success as a win- win situation. They are willing to help you in any way they can. They are ready to share their knowledge, expertise, experiences and strategies with you. You in turn should also observe them carefully, especially if you want to have what they have. Observe their lifestyle, their daily habits, their behavioural patterns, the way they think and act, the books they read, the materials they study, and so forth. Adopt all the positive and good habits that they possess, and implement them to create the life of your dreams.

Congratulations -- you are now one-third through your journey to success!

Now that you have cleared all the roadblocks you need to start creating a blueprint.
You need to have a set plan of how you will start creating everything that is going to happen in life. You need to have a step-by-step action plan that will move you closer to your dreams. You have to figure out what works for you the best, and move in that direction. They do not have to be giant steps. They can be small baby steps that will take you closer to your goals. The blueprint will help you achieve the life purpose that you have discovered. Once you put your full attention to

it, the universe will conspire in such a way that you will start attracting the right resources at the right time.

'Our goals can only be reached through a vehicle of a plan, in which we must fervently believe, and upon which we must vigorously act. There is no other route to success"
- Pablo Picasso

EXERCISE 5 - CLEARING ROADBLOCKS

LIST 5 REASONS THAT HAVE STOPPED YOU BEFORE FROM ACHIEVING WHAT YOU DESIRED

1. _____

2. _____

3. _____

4. _____

5. _____

Notes:

_____

_____

_____

_____

_____

_____

_____

_____

_____

_____

_____

_____

_____

_____

_____

_____

Notes:

_____

_____

_____

_____

_____

_____

_____

_____

_____

_____

_____

_____

_____

_____

_____

Notes:

_____

_____

_____

_____

_____

_____

_____

_____

_____

_____

_____

_____

_____

_____

_____

Notes:

_____

_____

_____

_____

_____

_____

_____

_____

_____

_____

_____

_____

_____

_____

_____

_____

CHAPTER 7

CREATING YOUR BLUEPRINT

What is a blueprint?

A blueprint is a design or a plan that is outlined to achieve the desired outcome.

You might wonder why you need a life blueprint. Up until now you have probably lived a life in a manner in which you face anything that comes your way. But now you need to change your way of thinking. You need to be in control of your life so you can manifest everything that you want in your life. You now have the power to choose, and hence you have the choice of what you want to include in your blueprint for your life. You now want to have a life that you have designed for yourself, and to be able to do that you need a clear plan.

You need to have a plan to achieve what you want

A clear blueprint helps you stay focused on the important activities that are in alignment with your goals and your life purpose. It helps you to maximize your energy and gain clarity. You are able to manage your energy and focus. Once you have a plan, you are able to accomplish a lot more without having to worry about insufficient time. It helps you to be more productive so that you can create a good balance between work and life.

A blueprint is like a road map that helps you stay on the track.

Your blueprint must be based on your dreams, your life purpose, your vision and your goals, but it need not be foolproof.

The important thing is that you have a plan of action. It is perfectly alright if it has some flaws in it. It need not be perfect; after all, the best way to learn is through your mistakes.

**" Failure is not the opposite of success, it is a part of success."
- Arianna Huffington**

Does not have to be foolproof

It is only through failures that we learn to be stronger. We can definitely learn from other people's past mistakes, but when we face failures ourselves we grow internally. Do not be afraid to fall; just pick yourself up and get back on the track leading to success.

May have to face failures

Never let failure get to your heart. Use failure as feedback. Never let it stop you. Never let failure steal you from your dreams. Take it as constructive criticism, and strive towards constantly improving your blueprint. Failure is not a step back or an obstacle, it is a learning opportunity that will help you determine your path to building your dream.

"I have not failed, I have just found 10,000 ways that don't work." - Thomas Edison

This famous quote by Edison teaches us a lot. It proves that you will succeed one day if you keep following your dreams and stay on the path. You do not want to have regrets at the end of your life. You want to be able to say proudly, "I gave it my best shot." Your determination will help you create the life you deserve. You need to be doing what needs to be done according to the plan, even when you do not feel like doing it. You must never give up. Stick to your plan as much as you can. I know that life will throw you some curves time and again, but if you have a strong *why*, you will come out victorious.

Be persistent

Be persistent in your journey towards creating a desirable life. Persistence always pays off. Never underestimate the power of persistence. Never let the odds keep you from the blueprint that you have created. You may have to change the plan sometimes, but never change your goals. Practice persistence in every aspect of your life. People who possess the quality of persistence are strong enough to face any challenges in life.

> **"Persistence is to the character of a man,
> that carbon is to steel." - Napoleon Hill**

Like any other, persistence is a quality that you can develop. Practice persistence.

In the book *Think And Grow Rich*, Napoleon Hill has written a chapter on how you can develop persistence. He says, you need:

1. A definite purpose backed by burning desire for its fulfillment
2. A definite plan expressed in continuous action
3. A mind closed tightly against negative and discouraging influences
4. A friendly alliance with one or more persons who will encourage you to follow through with both plan and purpose

Be consistent

It takes awareness and practice to acquire the quality of persistence. No matter how many times you fail, how many times you feel like giving up or feel discouraged, keep on going. The road may seem difficult first, but eventually it will get easier. The only people who never fail are the people who never try, and who do not pursue their dreams. If you stumble upon a roadblock, pause to brainstorm but never stop. You can think of other strategies and plans that will help you get to your goals. You can turn your failures from stumbling blocks to stepping stones. Commit to constant improvement and personal growth. Once you develop the inner strength, you can help others to grow and create the life they deserve.

> **"Persistence and determination alone are omnipotent"
> - Calvin Coolidge, Thirtieth President of the United States**

CONSISTENCY IS 🗝

SUREFIRE WAYS TO GET YOU CLOSER TO YOUR DREAMS AND GOALS

1. Constant Learning
2. Having mentors and coaches
3. Being a part of a Mastermind group
4. Having accountability partners
5. Networking

1. Constant Learning - For you to grow and succeed, you need to be learning constantly, reading good inspirational books, listening to motivational CDs, participating in events and seminars that will teach you how to get closer to your goals.

There are a lot of good non-fictional books out there, such as biographies, self-help and personal development books by great transformational leaders like my mentors Bob Proctor, Jack Canfield, Raymond Aaron, and many more.

Success is a journey. When you achieve your goals and create the life you deserve, it is not just what you have achieved but it is who you have become in the process that matters the most.

After reading this book and doing all the work that is needed in order to get what you want, you will transform into a being who will have more control of your thoughts, behaviour and actions.

"The more that you read, the more things you will know. The more that you learn, the more places you will go" - Dr. Seuss

2. Having mentors and coaches - The importance of having mentors and coaches is that they been there, done that. This means that they gone down the same path that you are on, and have had experiences that they can share with you. You can learn from their past mistakes. They will share their wisdom and knowledge with you, so that you can be on a fast track to success. Mentors will guide you through your entire journey, and lead you in the right direction.

You can have different coaches for different areas of your life, such as financial, relationship, health, business, and so on.

You need to seek these coaches and have complete trust that they will invest in you fully to see that you succeed. They will uplift you.

If you need more information on certain matters please do not ask your friends, co-workers, neighbours, relatives, family or anyone else who has no clue about it. It is fruitless asking for advice from people who have no idea about the issues or problems you are facing. You need to ask the right people!

One of the most important determinants of success is that you constantly seek guidance and advice from experts. Ask someone who has already done it successfully before.

"A mentor is someone who sees more talent and ability within you than you see in yourself, and helps bring it out of you" - Bob Proctor

3. Being a part of a mastermind group - In the book *Think and Grow Rich*, Napoleon Hill defines Mastermind as "coordination of knowledge and effort, in a spirit of harmony between two or more people, for the attainment of a definite purpose."

As a single person, you may or may not be able to achieve as much, but as a team you will definitely achieve a lot more than what you had set out for. You need to be selective of your Mastermind group. You need to include people who are aligned with your core values and principles, and who share the same vision as you. You need to share a common definite purpose with the individuals in your group.

The basic theory behind forming a Mastermind group is that more can be achieved in less time when individuals work together. The group meet on a regular basis, weekly, biweekly or monthly. Members share ideas, thoughts, plans, information, knowledge and resources. They also use feedback as an important part of the process for improvement. They have to be extremely truthful and honest with each other, and value each other's feedback.

By being part of an effective mastermind group, you will have more opportunities and resources.

The group is built on trust and confidentiality. Everything that is said or happens in the group stays within. You need to be very open and let your guard down. Most importantly, you need to feel safe in order to be vulnerable. You need to be absolutely comfortable being around people in the group.

The ideal size of a mastermind group is 6-8 people. If it is too small it loses its dynamics, and if it is too large it will probably lead to confusion and chaos. The meetings should be scheduled in such a way that every member has a turn to voice his/ her concern, to share their problems and also provide solution and feedback to others through brainstorming and asking clarifying questions. It should be a time-controlled meeting and must follow a proven format.

**"If you find you are weak in persistence,
surround yourself with a Mastermind group"
- Napoleon Hill (*Think and Grow Rich*)**

4. Having accountability partners - In addition to being a part of a mastermind group, you may also choose to work with an accountability partner. It could be one or more individuals, with whom you agree to work toward set goals. These could be different for each of the partners, but you hold each other accountable for meeting deadlines, achieving goals, and accomplishing tasks.

You mutually agree upon a set time each week for a phone call or meeting online, to make sure that you are following through on your plan of action. By doing this you become motivated, and you will make sure that the job you set out to do gets done. Reporting to your partner every week helps you to stay on track. It also helps you focus and manage your energy better, which leads to having more time during the day to complete all your tasks. You are then a lot more productive, and you get your job done on time.

You can also ask your partners their opinions, ideas and thoughts on matters that you may be dealing with at any given time. You can also ask them if they would be willing to share their contacts and resources, which would help you get results faster, and you can do the same for them in return. The key to a successful accountability relationship is partnering with someone who is committed to your success as well as their own.

"Accountability is the glue that ties commitment to the result"- Bob Proctor

5. Networking - Besides mentors and accountability partners, there are other people who may have the same dreams or are striving towards achieving the same goals as you. On the journey of creating the life you deserve, if business is one aspect that will help you get there, you must definitely network. You must get involved in plenty of networking events that will help you generate referrals to increase your business. You will meet like-minded individuals who share the same vision. The reason you must network is to build long-lasting relationships. The only way you can do that is through interaction and communication.

You will be presented with new opportunities that could take your life to the next level. Through networking you will be able to connect with influential and powerful people who are willing to help you get what you want. Having like-minded people to talk to gives you the opportunity to get advice on many aspects of your business and personal life.

"Your network will determine your net worth" - Jim Bunch

Notes:

_____

_____

_____

_____

_____

_____

_____

_____

_____

_____

_____

_____

_____

Notes:

_____

_____

_____

_____

_____

_____

_____

_____

_____

_____

_____

_____

_____

_____

_____

Swapna Ambegaonkar

Notes:

CHAPTER 8

AND ACTION!

"The Path To Success Is To Take Massive Determined Action"
- Tony Robbins

The most important step - take action

The most important step that differentiates the winners from the losers is that they take action. Action is the foundational key to success. Successful people are extremely action-oriented. Once have your dreams outlined, your vision defined and your goals set, the next most important step is to take action. You may have big plans, and designed a great blueprint for how you would like to create the life you desire, but if you do not have an action plan you are not going to be able to achieve anything big in life.

Do you have to be perfect in the action you take? No, you don't. In fact you may at times find that if something does not work the way it is supposed to, you have to change your actions.

When you take action you invariably start attracting all the right resources, people, and lots of other things that will take you in the direction of success. The Law of Attraction states "We attract whatever we choose to give our attention to--whether wanted or unwanted." This law is very accurate, but it will only be in effect if you act upon that which you wish to attract in life. You cannot just simply wait for things to appear by themselves. You need to take action!

"To wish for change, will change nothing; to make the decision to take action right now will change everything"
- Nick Vujicic

In order to take action you must be willing to ask. Ask for anything that you want to be successful. You may ask for help, for money, for expertise, anything at all that will get you on your path to success.

One of Jack Canfield's success principle states " Ask, Ask, Ask."

Just ask! Asking is the secret to success.

If taking action and asking is the most important step in achieving the life you deserve, why do people not take action?

Why do people not take action?

The main reason is FEAR. People are afraid to take action! People have the fear of asking! They have the fear of rejection and fear of failure. They even have the fear of success. They have the fear of looking foolish, and are afraid of what others might think of them.

There is a great book written by New York Times Best Selling author, Terry Cole- Whittaker titled, *What You Think of Me is None of My Business*. This is a great book, in which the author has written about how you should follow your inner path to achieve success and happiness, and not worry about what other people will think of you.

Face your fear and do it anyway

You need to get over your fear. Look at it this way: Before you ask, you do not have what you want, and if the answer is *no* after you ask, you still don't have it. So you had nothing to lose to begin with. For example, if you are looking to start a business and need money to do so, you ask the bank or other lenders. If their answer is *no*, you did not have the money in the first place, so you are no further behind. But if they say *yes* you are in a better situation than you were before. You should not assume that the answer is going to be *no*. You will not know unless you ask. You must always ask in a way that you expect to get what you have asked for. There is no harm in asking.

"You create opportunities by asking for them"
- Shakti Gawain

Learn to ask

When you ask someone for something, maybe he or she does not have what you are looking for, but could lead you to someone who does. This way you are opening new possibilities for yourself. When you ask, you need to be clear and specific on what you are asking for. For example, if you want more money, it is not enough to merely say "I want more money." You need to specify the amount and the time period. So you might want to ask, for example, "I want 10k dollars by December 31, 2017." When you put out a clear and specific intent, you get the desired result.

You need to be persistent in your asking. If your *why* is strong enough, you will ask repeatedly until you get it. Little kids are extremely good at asking repeatedly. They never give up until they get what they want. They may change their questions but they never give up on their goals. You need to be persuasive until you get what it is that you desire.

Another reason people are afraid to take action is because of their limiting beliefs and daily habits. Let us talk about limiting beliefs. These are the vivid images that people have created for themselves in their mind. The mind cannot tell the difference between a real and a vividly imagined event. People have certain beliefs about themselves, of the things they can or cannot do. These limitations lead to the fear of failure. If you have imagined in your head that you are going up to someone to ask for money, but are going get a no in return, you are going to be afraid to ask. This in turn causes you to be afraid to fail.

"In order to succeed, your desire for success should be greater than your fear of failure."- Bill Cosby

Learning from your mistakes

Failure is just another stepping stone to success. If you consider failure to be a part of success, and not opposite to it, you will be able to deal with adverse situations and failures a lot better. Consider a failure to be a learning experience. Learn from your past mistakes.

You should learn to take *no* for an answer and just move on. Keep on going until you have achieved your goals. Like Jack Canfield teaches in his events, when someone says *no*, you say *Next*. Just keep on doing this until you get a favourable response. Do not take a negative response personally. It has absolutely nothing to do with you. If you keep this in mind, you will be able to overcome all obstacles and succeed. On your journey to create the life you deserve, there will be a lot of rejection, but just keep in mind that it is a part of the exciting journey you are about to embark upon. If you have it clear in your mind that no matter what comes along you are determined to have the life you so desire, you will be able to jump over every hurdle that you encounter along the way.

Many famous people have had to face failures. But they let their failures inspire them to achieve great things in life. When you change your thoughts from negative to positive, you will start seeing more success than failure.

When an idea comes to mind just take action!

Don't wait to be ready to take action. If you wait until you have a foolproof plan, it might be too late. Once you start acting upon the ideas that you have, you will find yourself in a creative state of mind and will start attracting greater ideas and resources. Just take a leap of faith! We have this great intellect consisting of intuitive powers. Trust your instincts and just go for it! Learn to pay attention to your inner voice. This inner voice is your guidance on your journey. Listen to it and make a decision to act.

It does not matter if it is the right or the wrong decision. Just make a decision!

The vast majority of the people have trouble making decisions. They are afraid to make wrong decisions. It does not matter if you choose wrongly because you can always go back and change your decision. The important fact is that you make a decision. Unless you do that you will not move ahead. You will be stuck where you are, and that is the reason the majority of the people feel stuck in life, because of their inability to decide. People procrastinate. They add time. They put off things that they feel are difficult to decide on. By adding time you are only delaying your chances to succeed. The reason people procrastinate is because they are unsure of themselves. They are afraid to own their mistakes. They want to be perfect. There is no such thing as perfection. Always strive for progress, not perfection. Being perfect is a myth. When you strive to be perfect you fail to act. You must do everything in your power to obtain your desired outcomes, but then you need to let go.

"You must be able to win and lose with the same level of enthusiasm."
- Meir Ezra

You must carry out everything in your capacity to achieve what you want. Sometimes, however, you will not get the intended results. That's just the way the laws of the universe work. You have to accept what is, and not worry about the things that you cannot control. You need to remind yourself that you could get what you want, or something better. You must be willing to pay the price. You may have to give up certain things in order to acquire the life you desire. You may have to give up certain daily habits like watching TV, or give up some friends or relations who are toxic and pulling you down. You may even have to walk away from certain activities that are doing you no good, and not in alignment with your life purpose. All the sacrifices that you make, in the bargain for creating the life you deserve, are going to be totally worth it. Remember the pain or discomfort that you may experience from this is only temporary. It will pass. The benefits that you get, or the person you become while going through the process, are long-lasting. You are like the diamond that can shine only after burning the coal on the outside.

After going through and following all the steps outlined in this book, you will not only create the life you deserve but you will also transform into a being who will experience abundance in all areas of your life.

"Draw your line in the sand. Make your decision now and start taking action to really live your dream. By not taking bold steps to live your dream, not only are you missing out on fully living, but the world is missing out on the greatness you have to offer. Be bold!"
- Les Brown

EXERCISE 6 - TAKE ACTION

LIST 5 DAILY ACTION STEPS YOU WOULD TAKE TO GET YOU CLOSER TO YOUR GOALS :

1. _____

2. _____

3. _____

4. _____

5. _____

Notes:

_____

_____

_____

_____

_____

_____

_____

_____

_____

_____

_____

_____

_____

_____

_____

_____

Notes:

_____

_____

_____

_____

_____

_____

_____

_____

_____

_____

_____

_____

_____

_____

Notes:

_____

_____

_____

_____

_____

_____

_____

_____

_____

_____

_____

_____

_____

_____

Notes:

_____

_____

_____

_____

_____

_____

_____

_____

_____

_____

_____

_____

_____

_____

CHAPTER 9

ACKNOWLEDGING FEEDBACK

"The Most Powerful Single Modification That Enhances Achievement Is Feedback"
- John Hattie

You need to re-evaluate your plan

Now that you have a plan and have started taking action, you need to re-evaluate your plan every so often. You can do it monthly or every six months. This helps you see for yourself if you are going in the right direction toward your goals. It helps you focus and makes you aware if you are in alignment with your purpose. If at any point during your journey you feel that you are confused or in doubt, ask yourself this one very important question: "Is what I am about to undertake or what I am doing currently in alignment with my dreams, my vision and my goals?" If the answer is *no*, give up what is not working for you.

Change your actions, not your goals

You can always change your actions, but never change or give up on your goals. Re-evaluation of your action plan helps you refocus, and enables you to manage and channelize your energy better.

Listen to internal and external feedback

Once you get into action, you will receive a lot of feedback on your actions. This feedback can be either internal or external. Internal feedback is that which you get within yourself, your thoughts. You will have both positive and negative thoughts going through your head. How you respond to these thoughts is of utmost importance. You need to enhance the positive ones and get rid of the negative ones at once. You may encounter thoughts of self-doubt, your incapacities or scarcities in your life. Replace your reasoning of why you cannot do something with your *why*. When negative thoughts start crowding your mind, immediately focus on your dreams, the life you desire and want to have. This will help you shift your attention to your goals, and you will once again be on your way toward creating the life you deserve. You also need to pay attention to your intuitive feedback. Listen to your inner self. The best way to do this is by meditation. This will help you calm your mind, and you will be able to see things from a different perspective. Most of the time your gut feeling is correct. Learn to pay attention to it.

In addition to the internal feedback, you will receive a lot of external feedback. This is feedback provided by people around you, your family, your friends, and others with whom you associate. If these people in your life are not in alignment with your purpose, they are surely going to try and talk you out of this journey. They might give you a hundred reasons why this is a bad idea, and why you will not be able to achieve what you are trying to achieve. You will get lots of advice, suggestions, directions and even criticism. How you deal with these will depend on how strongly you want to create a better life for yourself. Some people may even try and offer their help, and this could be good or bad. There may be those who are genuinely trying to help, and of course there is nothing wrong with accepting help, as long as it is in congruence with your goals. I would once again like to emphasize the importance of association with the right like-minded positive people, and removing toxic people from your life. If you are open to receive feedback and advice from others, it should be from individuals who understand your journey. These people are either those who recognize and relate to your dreams and goals, or they are mentors and teachers who guide you through this journey.

Improving through feedback

It is very important to ask for feedback. Feedback helps you improve. It keeps you in check with your self. Good feedback is the key to improvement.

"Feedback is a free education to excellence. Seek it with sincerity and receive it with grace."
- Ann Marie Houghtailing

Feedback through results is one of the best types of feedback you can get. It could be positive or negative. We prefer positive feedback and are extremely happy to receive it. Positive feedback could be a raise, a promotion, a satisfied client, happy spouse, happy children, inner peace, merits, awards, more money, improved health. These results are indicators that we are on the right path and we need to continue what we are doing.

Get comfortable with external feedback

We do not like negative feedback, and we tend to ignore it. Negative feedback could be lack of results, loss of income, unhappiness, conflicts, criticism, complaints, irate customers, pain, and obesity. Although tough, we have to acknowledge this, and strive to achieve better. Negative feedback teaches us where we lack, and the areas we need to improve in. It tells us if we are headed in the right direction.

The moment you get negative feedback you must at once stop and analyze your actions. This is valuable information and helps you stay on course. You need to get comfortable with receiving external feedback. You should be willing to ask for it.

People may not want to give their honest feedback as they may not want to hurt you, but you have to be brave enough to ask for their honest feedback as it will only help you to do better. You may have set certain limitations for yourself unknowingly, and you have to ask to be able to get rid of them so that you function at your maximum potential.

When you avoid asking for feedback you are only hurting yourself by not being able to see the true picture. Do not be afraid to ask for corrective feedback. Constructive criticism is very helpful in being more effective and productive. You must appreciate the feedback you get, as this going to be critical in your journey to success.

3 ways to improve from feedback:

1. Accept the feedback
2. Find something in it to agree with
3. Determine how it can help you in the future

As Elon Musk says, "I think it is very important to have a feedback loop, where you are constantly thinking about what you have done and how you could be doing it better. I think that is the single best piece of advice, constantly think about how you could be doing things better and questioning yourself."

Learn to respond, not react to feedback

It is very important that you pay attention to feedback. Do not ignore it. Once someone gives you feedback, especially unfavourable feedback, make sure you do not react to it. Take the feedback in good stride and reflect upon it. Sometimes when we think about it instead of just reacting to it harshly, especially if it seems very negative at first, we tend to respond better. By responding you may be able to see the hidden truth that could be to your advantage. How you respond to feedback can make all the difference in how successful you are at achieving your goals. You just need to acknowledge it and keep moving forward. You have done the best you could, so gain insight from it. Be aware of all the lessons that you learnt, and be grateful to others for delivering their feedback. Take whatever serves you well, forgive the rest and move on. Refocus on your vision and commit to constant improvement.

"The natural response to evaluation is to feel judged. We have to mature to a place where we respond to it with gratitude, and love feedback." - Henry Cloud

Notes:

_____

_____

_____

_____

_____

_____

_____

_____

_____

_____

_____

_____

_____

_____

Notes:

_____

_____

_____

_____

_____

_____

_____

_____

_____

_____

_____

_____

_____

_____

_____

_____

Notes:

_____

_____

_____

_____

_____

_____

_____

_____

_____

_____

_____

_____

_____

_____

_____

CHAPTER 10

CELEBRATING YOUR LIFE

"LIFE SHOULD NOT ONLY BE LIVED,
IT SHOULD BE CELEBRATED." - Osho

Celebrate your success -- big or small

Why is it important to celebrate your success?

Now that you are on your last chapter of this book, you are on your way to success!

Congratulations for following through on all the exercises outlined in this book. If for some reason you have not completed the exercises, I urge you strongly to do so.

The exercises given after each chapter are extremely important, as they will help you create the path to your success.

You now have a dream. You have discovered your purpose and clarified your vision. You have set your goals. You have also cleared all your roadblocks and taken action by facing your fears, and you have learnt to listen to feedback and use it to your advantage. All these steps followed in exactly the same order as described in the book along with the exercises will surely help you in your journey within, to create the life you deserve!

The order in which the chapters are written is very crucial. It is highly recommended you follow the same order if you want to achieve your goals and thus bring about a transformation in your life and business.

The reason you should celebrate your success, either big or small, is because it increases your self-esteem and boosts your self-confidence. Once you start seeing the desired results, you need to acknowledge them by celebrating. This helps you to start believing in yourself, which in turn will lead you to achieving greater results.

By celebrating you are validating yourself. You are congratulating yourself and acknowledging the fact that you are capable of a lot more than you think. Self-validation is a great process as it increases your faith in yourself and confirms in your mind that you are born to do great things.

Most of the time you are constantly seeking approval from others. You are often asking the opinions of family members, relatives, friends, co-workers, community, neighbours and so on. You feel good if they agree with and approve of your actions. Your happiness depends solely on what they say. From now on you need to stop doing that, and start seeking your own approval. It is good to ask for opinion and feedback, as I mentioned in the previous chapter. In fact it is important that you do so, but do not be heavily dependent on it. Do not base your happiness and joy on that. Start validating yourself. When you achieve something that you have been striving for, congratulate yourself.

Appreciation is the key to success

Start by self-appreciation. It is very important that you practice self-love every day. Only when you love and appreciate yourself will you be able to see the good in others. Stop criticizing yourself. Look for the good in you. Admire your own qualities.

Unfortunately, right from childhood we have been told that we should not be selfish, and that it is wrong to put ourselves first. This is the way we have been programmed, and hence we believe that it is wrong to appreciate ourselves. This is one of the reasons why we start seeking others' approval. But think of it this way: if you take good care of yourself and practice self-love daily, you will be in a better position to take good care of your loved ones and those in your life. To give you an example, if you are flying in an airplane and the oxygen in the cabin suddenly drops, you are asked to put on your mask first and then help the person next to you, especially if it's your child. The same way, if you look after your health, your happiness, and fulfill your needs first, you will be more effective in doing that for your loved ones.

Along with self-love and acceptance, you need to start appreciating others. Start looking for everything that is good about a person or situation. Start developing a positive mental attitude. Get rid of the negativity and only look for things that you can start appreciating. It is not easy to begin with; hence it should be a daily practice. You can begin by appreciating every little thing around you. Maybe start with your spouse or your kids. Start appreciating the house in which you live or the place where you work. You may not be satisfied with where you live or work, but once you start appreciating all that you already have, you create a mindset of abundance. You start attracting all the good things, and all the right things in your life. The law of the universe starts working in your favour and gives back to you all of life's wonderful gifts. Get rid of all the complaining, blaming and negativity from your life and see for yourself how beautiful your life turns out to be. You now vibrate in the highest frequencies that attract happiness, wealth, compassion, good heath, satisfaction, and everything else that you need to create the life you desire.

Express gratitude daily

The law of attraction states "In order to receive good, you must give out good." You must give positive in order to receive positive. It has been seen that most people who are "the givers" have a tough time receiving. This means that you should not only give lovingly, but you must also know how to receive graciously.

I have seen people who are not comfortable when they get a compliment. In fact they try their best to justify why they are not worthy of receiving it. They try and put themselves down. They give many reasons why they are unfit for the validation.

Just learn to say "Thank you!" No matter how big or small is the action for which you have received the compliment, just graciously thank the person for it. When you accept validation you are now vibrating in the frequency where you are able to give more. Do not discount yourself ever.

It is also very important to express gratitude daily. The best way to do this is to keep a gratitude journal. I have been doing this myself for more than two years now, and it has helped me tremendously in my life and business. Start by journaling 10 things that you are grateful for each day. You can do this as part of your morning ritual. By doing this you are putting yourself in a state of appreciation, and you will then start attracting more great things in your life. It helps you get rid of all the negativity, hatred and resentment that you may harbour within yourself. In fact every time you feel resentful of something or someone, look for the good or the positivity in that person or situation. It is not easy to do at the beginning, but it will become easy with continued practice. Make gratitude a habit in your life.

Sanjana Ambegaonkar, the award-winning author of the book *The Art Of Appreciation: how to appreciate everything you have and take nothing for granted*, has outlined six simple steps that you can take to make gratitude a natural part of your daily routine, so you can attract more joy and abundance in your life:

Step1: Take 7 minutes every morning to write down everything you appreciate

Step 2: Make a conscious effort to appreciate at least 3 people every day

Step 3: Play the appreciation game

Step 4: Carry a physical token of gratitude in your pocket such as a heart- shaped stone, crystal or some other small item

Step 5: Remember to appreciate the smallest blessing you have

Step 6: Appreciate yourself

To learn more about how you can enhance your daily appreciation, read the book.

The following is an excerpt from an article by my mentor, Jack Canfield:

"Appreciation is one of the highest emotional states you can experience. When you cultivate gratitude, you are able to feel true joy and contentment, no matter what you have or don't have in your life. And since the Law of Attraction states that like attracts like, when you are grateful for what you already have, you will naturally attract more for which you can be grateful."

Share your successes and inspire people

The most important step you can now take is to share your success! You have read this entire book, followed up on your dreams, taken action, and are on the path to creating the life you deserve. This is the time for celebration. By sharing your success story, you could possibly inspire others to do the same. This was the purpose of my writing this book. It was to be able to share my secrets, and knowledge that I have learnt and acquired from my mentors, to help you create the life you have always desired but for some reason did not either know how or were unable to take the required steps to do so.

Now that you have the knowledge yourself, once you have achieved the life of your dreams, I urge you to share your stories and your experiences with others, so that they can start creating the life they deserve. Believe me, by doing so it will only enhance and enrich your life. So start sharing your success and inspiring others to live the life of their dreams.

Remember it is not only about the goals or the dreams that you achieve in the end, but who you become in the process of achieving them that matters. For you to get what you want, you need to change. You need to grow internally. You cannot do the same thing and expect better results. You have to take certain actions; you have to change your habits, your behaviour. You have to evolve into a better being, for only then you will be capable and worthy of the life you deserve.

This is your journey! It is the journey within yourself to grow, expand, be more aware, be more creative, face your fears and discover who you really are in the process of creating the life you truly deserve!

My friend, I will leave you now with one last quote:
"Sometimes in life we become so focused on the finish line
that we fail to find joy in the journey."
- President Dieter F. Uchtdorf

This is not the end, but the beginning of....Your Journey Within!

Notes:

_____

_____

_____

_____

_____

_____

_____

_____

_____

_____

_____

_____

_____

_____

_____

Notes:

_____

_____

_____

_____

_____

_____

_____

_____

_____

_____

_____

_____

_____

Notes:

_____

_____

_____

_____

_____

_____

_____

_____

_____

_____

_____

_____

_____

_____

_____

_____